# Severn Bridge

## New and Selected Poems

BARBARA HARDY

Shoestring  Press

Typeset by The Midlands Book Typesetting Company, Loughborough
(01509 210920)
Printed by Quorn Selective Repro Loughborough (01509 213456)

Published by Shoestring Press
19 Devonshire Avenue, Beeston, Nottingham, NG9 1BS
(0115) 925 1827

ISBN: 1 899549 54 4

east midlands
arts
making creative
opportunities

Shoestring Press gratefully acknowledges financial assistance from
East Midlands Arts

# Severn Bridge

To my daughters, Julia and Kate Hardy

and warm thanks to John Ackerman, Isobel Armstrong,
Michael Baron, Bland Crowther, Martin Dodsworth,
Jim Doolan, Janet El-Rayess, Diana Godden, Sam Hynes,
Graham Handley, Hannah Hobshaum-Kelly, John Lucas,
Peter Lewis, Bill Nathan, Sue Roe, Michael Slater,
Jennifer Tanner, J.P. Ward,
and Birkbeck Poetry Workshop

# Contents

# Severn Bridge

## Sweets

I walked again the way we went to school
from 22 Cradock Street up Carlton Terrace
where every day I counted cracks in walls
played Daddy Daddy Can I Cross the Water
and the Big Ship Sailed on the Ally Ally O
to Heathfield up the stone steps by the Green
where I picked bitter wormwood and blanched barley
near the corner house where Valerie Williams lived
whose parents talked fast Welsh in front of the children
past the quarry where we dared Alpine climbs
and Peggy Petters told me the facts of life
while I gaped and gasped no-one would do it
near steep Primrose Hill whose iron rails remain
a bit bent now where we hung like wobbly bats
telling tall tales about the gory stain
and my tightroping brother cracked his new front tooth
just across from the Spanish chestnut tree
felled long ago but the grassy slope we searched
for skeleton leaves and tender nuts still green
by Cromwell Street where Glenys James told me
boys liked big breasts and her old grandfather
recited all Poe's *Raven* in deep solemn tones
as we listened rapt and nearly died laughing
then Norfolk Street where the school's still standing
Terrace Road School with its weathervane veering
gold glitter on a tower above the playgrounds
high flights of steep sharp steps we jumped
where bold as a heroine from the Abbey school
I punched a rude boy teasing Valerie
as we played orphans and cruel guardians
and I sulked when Miss Clemonts sent me out for talking
saying I couldn't be a fairy in her Christmas play
where we had singing games with Loopy Loo
ran out to icecream carts and raspberry vinegar
or an old hunched man swopping rags for goldfish
near the twin sweetshops on opposite streetcorners
Mrs Davies for the boys and for us Mrs Lily
yellow sherbetsuckers and cocobutternuts
pied peardrops flinty mints and lucky packets
windows filled with everlasting sweets.

1

# Mitching

O what's become of all the cheeky boys
who used to wolfwhistle and wink at us
dawdling along the primrose path to school?

They're dead as doornails now those lovely boys
their blue eyewhites all bleary and veined
their apple cheeks lapsed into flabby jowls

their ghosts playing truant in the skulls
of randy grandfathers taking the air
blind to the kind smiles of tidy wives
and wondering where their flighty girls are gone.

## Grandpa's Stories

When we meet by and by
to feast in that chapel's paradise
you invoked for Sunday grace
as long as there was hot dinner

we'll play
Fox and Geese
Tip-It or Knockout Whist
you sometimes said No
there's a bone in my leg
even your refusals were riddles.

A Christmas crown of sugar flowers
flowed from your fingers
gold blobs of dough
bobbing in frothy fat
lobbed in a ladle
stabbed with scissors and crammed with jam.

The squire sent brandy to the bakehouse
for his cake
you drank it down then breathed
into the rich mix.

Tommy Rogers of Watershill
wits turned by the full moon
threatened to kill you
look over there you said
and tipping him out of the trap
don't forget the baker.

Your father playing cards
with a stranger at the inn
dropped the ace of spades
and bending down
saw the hoof under the table.

# Father and Daughter

He came back and his face was the face
I'd looked at so hard through the long childhood
in the middle of my mother's mantelpiece
and in certain dreams.

He read me Grimms' fairytale
of the robber bridegroom
suddenly stopped before the end
fearing and fixing my fear.

Until we grew out of god
we said our prayers every night
for his safe return home
through stormless seas.

I boasted to my Jewish friends
about my newfound Jewish blood
never knew my grandfather's name
or his port of departure.

Once like father and child
we trembled on the edge of quarrel
temper unsheathed and flashed for a second
then we smiled like civilised strangers

and I saw his shrunk face in the coffin
woke in the night to hear him laughing
as he sat up straight in his graveclothes
I'm dead but I won't lie down

bought a black hat for the funeral
ordered red roses from my mother
who carried red roses at your wedding
and I looked down into your grave.

## Julia and the Time Machine

She pushes back her hair behind her ears
As I have seen her do over the years
Staring beyond me with a slaty gaze
While she talks about an experiment
On the child's sense of times and distances.

Piaget says space is a still of time
And time's the name we give to moving space,
Julia has designed a time machine
Using a beach buggy and forklift truck
Green and red matchbox cars to run a race.

Handles and rods and cogs and strings engage
To start and stop the toys at different times
To push and pull the toys at different speeds
While children grouped according to their age
Observe the permutations of the game.

She questions them about time and distance.
Their answers are not what you might expect
Their answers differ from the ones we'd give
Taking it all in with a rapid glance
If we were tested by that time machine.

After she hurtled out of her first space
At more than the anticipated speed
I measured time and space on her behalf
Clocks ticked to mark her sleep and her waking
Maps drew round the contours of her need.

As she started to count days and nights
Spelling through the hard alphabet of time
Tomorrow was the word she soon got right
But seemed reluctant to mouth yesterday
Although in time she had to tell the time.

The nursery cuckoo clock has lost its chime
But today as you talk and look ahead
In your own time going your own sweet way
I see you as the child who shared my space
Embrace you as the child I gave to time.

## Conversation Piece

I was going to tell you that
she got a kick out of being ninety
you'd have smiled at the kin and kissing
the room rich with wishes
I'd have liked some help with the champagne.

I started to tell you about
the child's eyes lit with recognition
of the calves feeding at the manger
when we took her into the barn
at Christmas.

I wanted to tell you how
I went to the new gallery at Dijon
they've got the Stilllife with Saucepan
which tore the skin off our eyes
as we saw paint for the first time.

Another onesided conversation
so much seems to have happened
and I'm dying to tell you all about it
you've got every reason for silence
don't leave me to do all the talking.

## Pollen Count in Cwmdonkin

In my childhood gardens
I scent danger
air dense with piercing gold dots
over the levelled dip and ghost waters

where reservoir glinted through bushes and railing
as we talked and walked round the dark circle
rubbing bay and laurel in our palms
rhyming footsteps and kisses

air thick with killing green motes
cutter wheeling on the steep lawn
where we lay in the long grass
gazing at ants, eyes, daisies,
sucking stalks, lips, clover,
drinking down love in big draughts

no trouble with breathing
in those aphrodisiac springs.

This year's pollen is heavy
this year's May is heady for me
I gasp and choke on love's potion.

## Ditch End

We four
file along the dyke
   by the old seawall
     scrawled
with yellow lichen

under a hunter's moon

its looking glass
   our brimming marsh.

## The Stream

Our threshold was a mossy bridging stone
you crossed the stream to get to the front door
welcomed by a sound of running water.

As the wild ponies whinnied in their dreams
and owls hunted in Cwm Ivy Woods
we slept and woke to sounds of running water.

It got mixed up with all the garden noise
children and birds in conversation
and backchat from the sound of running water.

They made the road and took the bridge away
forcing the vivid torrent underground
to run invisible down to the sea

and when I stand to listen by the gate
I can hear the sound of running water.

# The Fox and the Duck

I walk down to the shore at daybreak
And you cross my path, old softstepper,
Just by the Tor where we've often smelt you
Making tracks for your earth and cubs,
Back from the saltmarsh and watermeadows
Cradling a mallard in your mouth.

Surprised by me you drop the duck
Present me with your proper prey,
Averting eyes and quickening trot
To become a part of the browning bracken
As I pick up the unmarked cooling body
To make a dinner of your breakfast.

I sigh for the green and the nightblue pinions,
The pearly fluff of the tender breast feathers,
While with knowing hand I pluck the plumage
Till he lies there limp in a pimpled skin,
Killed by you and eaten by me,
You red beauty, bloodbrother.

# Farmer Paske's Land

A small round talkative man with a dirty laugh
he took me off the heavy potato lifting
and taught me how to drive the Fordson tractor
offering the freedom of his fertile acres.
I learnt to make furrows parallel
pull out the ploughshare at the proper place
and love the hubbub of the engine.

Summer was humming along as I plotted my patterns
when I felt a sudden jar against the blade
put on the brake and clambered out to find
a mole on its back waving short skinny legs
bright blood oozing from a little gash.

I stared down and made up my mind
to get a heavy stone with a sharp edge
picked one up, weighed it in my hand
shut my eyes and opened them again
to kill it with one quick bash on the neck
then I carried it to the hedge and buried it
in the earth of the twenty acre field.

# Cock Pride

Out of the blue you come with a crash,
you smash the still life outside the window,
flowering currant in lip-pink bunches
coaltits posed in pierrot masks
and green shoots on the bramble frieze
by the ironmould glitter from last autumn,
you dash your rose breast against the glass,

cock chaffinch in fighting fever
flying your chestnut and slate-blue colours
flaunting wingspan and darting beak
rapt, righteous, and bent on killing
the untouchable and matchless twin
mirrored there in a shimmering mirage,
hover for hover and lunge for lunge.

We shout at you with scarecrow reason,
Narcissus love-crossed to destruction,
we hang black cloths outside the window
till you take the war to another pane
and we search in the morning for the body
to find only a red smudge on the glass
with the bird on the bank all set for battle.

# The Light Heart

As ice melts
senses sharpen

to the fretted disc
of a morning moon
and the leathery flap
of lapwing

and as air softens
I bear the weight
of your shut sight
and hearing

a stone
in the breast

ballast

for a light heart.

# The Beach

These sands shift every season
flattening the heave of that bank
beyond the old lug and cockle beds
wind tossing high in plumey spouts
to choke the pool by the Tor
where the children learnt to swim
shaving off dunes to bare the clay
burying marramgrass and seaholly

gulls yelp over black musselrocks
by the cast-iron lighthouse
surf pours out its unmeasured roar
waves smash on the glassy shore
paired shelduck swing on ropes of air
rainbow tendril and brittle star
share the tideline with oranges and lemons
floated up from the Mediterranean.

My steps rubadub on sandribs
overprinting the delicate characters
carved by wave and seabird claw
I admire the shore's obscure rasp and rustle
languages of curlew and lark
hieroglyphs of wind and sand
as I stand between drowning and dryness
mine and theirs.

# Driftwood

Dawdling along the tideline he picks up driftwood,
bleached branches, splinters, rusty logs,
rough crumbly lumps, pine pieces, tarred blocks,
orangebox, doorpanel and carved chairleg,
sticks, spools and flakes of oar go into his sack
to be lugged up the lane and burnt for winter warming.
Intent on the grey waves he feels the glow of flame.

She kneels in front of the grate and picks up driftwood,
layers brittle sticks on cinder and paper
to build an intricate airy pyramid
spitting sparks and curling saffron fang
flaring and deepening into a heart of gold,
aquamarine and lapis of the salt stuff.
Stretching hands to the blaze she shivers on the shore.

## The Cherry Tree

Two lie under the cherry tree.

He lies easy
glances rising without care
where through lifting leaves and branches
after the usual flowerfall
all is given up to green
leaf overlapping leaf to darker green
leaf shadowing leaf to deeper green
while light shuttles between
and a convenient mild wind weaves
the leaves to shifting shapes and spaces
lacing frayed vein and threading
shreds of worn sapstream into fine frets
in a season's soft nets of shade and light
he lies easy.

She forbids light
to pierce lids tightening
on a tearstung darkness
as she recalls all the flushed flower fallen
shattered to scatter on the grass
leaving the torn calyx to hang threads
shredded by a persistent cool wind
which unmakes the clear spearshaft of the leaf
breaks the sappy stem's wholeness
dulls to monotones of brown and green
boughs and stripped sprigs
twigs heavy with heads of tossed bloom
luxuriant in the declining nostalgias
of her night
she forbids light.

The cherry tree stirs in its wind.

## Estuary

Sewin
elbowing
sheer muscle
in river skin
cowparsley and meadowsweet
starring grass
clotted rose flesh
scarring a snake's mesh
two gulls lit underwing
surf pouring hard
on sand's glass
winds backing tide
lift dunes
shift bank
bring an ocean
to the brink
of dryness.

# Llanmadoc Down

I have the contours and face by heart
stacked stones and circles of the iron age fort
scrolled bracken and red earth
know from every point of my compass
assuming each weather's fashion
to try the styles of a cold passion

woaded heather or russet bracken
compose hearts' blood-lapse
colouring griefs and births
sea-fog and moonless night figure emptiness
warm renewals of embrace
glint in the never out of season gorse

we scramble for a spring day in Rhossilli
climb down to Bluepool at August's low tide
rainproofs round waist and pockets of picnic
first-foot the highest ridge to sight Worms Head
January sunset dipping red
stage our seasons' story

days you must take ocean on trust
viewing gaps fill up with mist
moralise crag and cairn
catch breath when larks wind up an air
fox runs or rooks fly at a sparrowhawk
shine on sea-edge maps peninsula

but to observe the foursquare tormentil
lamb's bleached ribcage on the hill
or fingered scrawls in piled limestone
is to feel the hill's creatures hold their own
as when we form the manshape from a name
new stars move in to discompose the frame.

# Mrs Jenkins of Gelli Aur

The sign offered beans and homegrown tomatoes
so we lifted the catch on a grass-green gate
to meet Mrs Jenkins in her flowered pinnie
blue eyes fixed on the children's bare feet
but her gaze and voice sweetened to ask us in
patting Eira the white cat who slept in a cupboard
then wiping pink fingers on a clean cloth
she poured glasses of lemonade and sloe gin.

Not one of the godly who press blessings on you
she was positive God turned water to wine
greened her fingers and rooted her cuttings
put his thumbprint on showers and shine
and backed her vendetta with the la-di-da vicar
who took down the old falls from the pulpit
changed the hymn-tunes and neglected his flock
till they left church for good Mr Lloyd in the chapel.

We watched a sun set behind the Worms Head
found bloody cranesbill and viper's bugloss
she told me the name of the Rainy Rocks
and fields called by shapes of W and Hatchet
gave me white lilac and guelder rose
quickthorn for a gap where the sheep shoved through
a giant puffball that popped up on her lawn
and a holly when my first grandchild was born.

In her wellies and shiny-red leatherette coat
she nipped over seven stiles to Fairyhill
roused us before dawn one cold Boxing Day
to track badger-diggers in Cheriton Woods
righteously beat down a blocked right-of-way
and once as we walked to Whitford Spit
showed me three green woodpeckers lit by sun
and a red fox jumping the dunes.

# The Whitford Light

Lambing time
hold the dogs and shut the gate
sloe's snowy in the breaking spring
of these high hedges
never done with blossoming
scent of bramble and burnet rose
become taste of fruit
and campion's pink in late December.

Swing the farm's kissing-gate to remember
Mrs Ward's jet fringe and grin
as she twirled her black goat on a long string
his wicked yellow eyeslits winking
down the lane the fox crossed
dropping his duck for our dinner
where once at bat-time
we saw the man in a grey cloak.

Pick a summer path to the sea
thread wild thyme and dewberry
on the straight stony track
or skirt the salt marsh ebb and flood
sea-lavender, samphire and yellow-flag pod
where the ponies munch and suck
desolate pools on the way to the hide
and always the sweet-sour stink of the mud.

The north-west wind blows all year round
lifting and shifting the dunes
riffling the blanched marramgrasses
above the tide-line of rainbow plastic
where I sat in a shipwrecked armchair
watching oyster-catchers feeding
a single cormorant eyeing the ripples
from our airy cast-iron lighthouse

that crests white water or stands high and dry
in its street of purple cobbles
elegant and never manned
no kind light blinking
no ladder to the rusted delicate gallery
a hundred years old when we came here
they wanted to take it to California

and once in our midnight kitchen window
we saw its watery yellow beam winking.

# Gregynog Spring

As these first frail locust leaves
fire pale flames of amber

the huge yew hedge zigzags its glitter
serrated like perfect piecrust

wild geese strut in ungainly courtship
trumpeting hilarious heats of spring

a distant line of unmelted snow
sharpens the horizon


# The Fairings

Purple amethyst
drop
broochpin
twisted gold ring

blood
dart or noose

I get the gist
as he's carted off
for bandaging

I knew my dust
would get thirsty.

The fairings
are turning against us.

## The Comforters

Friends with flowers
swarm round
hotfoot from living
deadset against grieving
they hum with love

as once more greensick
she makes old bones
where love burbled in the belly
like a hot bird.

Death knew better
his bald head shone
he leaned on a stone
in his hand a cup
in his teeth a feather.

# Three Dreams

In the first dream
we were touching
nothing was said
bitter weather
but two in bed
close together

In the next dream
we were talking
wind dropped to whisper
my longing
your soft answer
no returning

In the last dream
we were fighting
winter backlighting
one stunted tree
discord of shouting
arms and hearts empty

Oh love
I wish it was bedtime
and everything easy

## Incense

I speak to you still
into silence.
If you could hear and answer there
beyond this pulse
of lip and ear
I could not hear.
You were the one who heard voices.

In our room there
was a view of valley and hill,
I listened still
when you spoke of air stirred
as the god passed
a bird in darkness.
I never caught a whiff of godhead.

All I have still
after this death
is a longing so like prayer
that if a god were near
he might drink his incense from my breath.

# In the Brompton Cemetery, 1950–94

There may be a name here for my next grandchild
among the headstones and springy grass
where we pushed our first pram past
the mild Victorian dead
Violet, Bertha, Hubert, Everard
railed in iron rectangles
praised for quiet and public rectitude
over whose virtue the ivy tangles

through the cream stone curving colonnade
whose in-and-out cool pillared shade
Cocteau's smart New Look Death may tread highheeling
over shelved dead crammed in catacombs
one grey granite slab still flowering
with praise from German and English admirers
fresh bouquets and encores for Richard Tauber's
bold voice to stir the silence of the grave

by rock-and-reeling Stanley Spencer tombs
that art deco angel who has lost her head
swords and guns arming the bandaged dead
zeppelin shot down in spiralled flames
sexton-mocking fresh foxholes
anchors and crosses and broken pillars
picnic tables for glum crows or flighty squirrels
hide-and-seek in little marble rooms.

# A Glass Bowl: Deganwy

On the sill a cutglass bowl of fruit
Left overnight to marry juice and colour
New moons of oranges and apples
Lit still life for a sweet tooth to savour.

A window's wide eye opened to the west
In a moist air the Snowdon hills showed clear
That lucky horseshoe where we climbed
To kissing-games and vows of playing house.

Of many fragile household gods
This is one I try to piece together
To hold the fruit we peeled and cut and left
For a last course in an early love-feast.

We ran down honeymoonstruck from those hills
Threw a blue cloth on a pink painted table
Piled high the first fruits in a crystal chalice
To eat together with our silver spoons.

## Ripe Apricots

Heat burned that August morning
when we left the train at Sens
stranded by the strike
to stretch out on a steep field's slope
and find a river at our feet.

Grey turrets standing in a bend of water,
solid walls softening in a calm shimmer,
Villeneuve-sur-Yonne, the inn tranquil,
outside our window the river ripple,
inside the grateful dark
of a room with red tiles cool to the foot.
At Joigny the streets twisted uphill
people talked on their doorsteps all night
we lay awake in a windowless heat
at dawn were shown a tangled garden
and said we would come back.
Yellowgreen wine at the hotel in Chablis
with mustard spread on paradisal bread
as we waited ravenous for coq-au-vin.
On the Feast of the Assumption
we were picking green walnuts
in the high vineyards
a shout warned us of thunder.
Bulging flies buzzed at our eyes
and emerald lizards flipped along the stones
by roads where my sandals stuck and melted,
long white straight roads pointing us on
as fatigue struck and words dried
I asked for history
you talked about the Persian wars
till the hot gates opened
on the heat of our walking.

Once we slept through the middle of the day
under a tree, waking to find ripe apricots —
the only ones you ever liked —
falling on us and all round
in the dry shadowed ground where we lay.

The barrows are piled high with fruit this season,
it's a good year for apricots.
I've had them drop soft into my mouth.

# The Plums

The air glittered
as I opened the window
to look into the quiet street
and let in the sun

when I saw under the sill
on the warm stone of the wall
yellowing plums
hanging heavy

so when you came in
I showed you the fruit
and you leaned out
to pick them

for us to eat with the wine
biting together
into the almost ripe
glassy flesh.

## Fontenay

An afternoon between two nights
time to be filled, time on my hands
to be spilled, in neutral spaces,
time to walk there and back before dark
certain of times and places
I drank deep draughts of fine air.

A roadsign pointed me the way
up the valley to Fontenay
climbing I counted kilometres,
watched my step as ice hardened
kept to the rough verges.
The abbey's mass loomed through a clear arch.

I stooped and took off my shoes to cross.
The bell banged in that still air
and a woman came, not expecting a visitor,
no, I was not disturbing her
it was her work, hers and her husband's
it was private property and one must stay with the guide.

She wrapped her black cardigan closely round her,
yes, I was a visitor, English not German,
come on foot and alone from Montbard,
had read about the abbey in the Michelin,
the road was quiet and the ice bad,
yes, we had Cistercian houses in England.

The natural earth of the huge nave,
the crusader and his wife in their shared stone,
the virgin's famous dimpled smile,
twinned pillars in the cloisters,
cells, dormitories, and workshops for each trade,
warm room for the scribes' cold fingers,

the house held massive presences,
no blank or neutral surface
no space there for my images
but the assertion of its strength and grace
beside the natural grace and strength of love.
I would walk back barefoot across the ice.

## Uncertainties of the Eye: At the Tate

It is theirs and all about them
they ease into possession
its dazzle strikes everywhere they look
sun streams through blue windows
on redchecked breakfast tables
facet of fruitskin and fishscale glistens
cold stones put out their hands
flesh sleeps softened by water
they run in and out of the frames
where cups and pots keep company
the tiptoe dancer never trembles
marble can mime embraces
and a glossy angel blessing the washerwomen
offers these altars without gods
for the midsummer marriage.

It is fun on Sunday mornings
three fat girls skip in a heavenly gutter
bronze monsters provide peepholes
to expose the heavy petting of the doves
as you tease Giacometti's stick insects
assemble Picasso's massive jigsaws
stare out Modigliani's blue-eyed boy
blow at mobiles and blink at dizzy Rileys
wham go the rockets in the dotty comics
and the daisyshirted dead clamber from toybox tombs
dazed or dangle over headstones
till you are stilled by the faded dancer
then by piercing a rainbow patchwork
stir up the spiralling snail
riddles for the growing eye.

In a room at Camden Town the woman
stares at an ageless portrait on the wall
the man has a glass before him on the table
a bored Olympia sprawls on her plinth
the cellist perfect in evening dress
stands impassive like her silent instrument

31

as Christ's hand grasps at its shadow
while nonchalant angels gape at open windows
the lipsticked ATS woman looks ahead
not far from the dead sea of wrecked warplanes
a bespectacled painter lolling detumescent
eyes his wife's genitals next to a lump of meat
the soldiers at Rye have twisted faces
and Rothko's enclosing walls are red and purple.

But the gods and goddesses of the galleries
do not speak of our history or their own
asserting a paradise never entered or lost
their frames repel the intruder
lover and child and loser
the brittle eyes of the glassy angel
are made of the same stuff as wings and washed linen
stony surfaces do not feel their smoothness
Sickert's gazing woman has no face
the taut dancer needs neither nerve nor muscle
the claw of the dove is four thin scratches
and Morandi's fluted vessels contain nothing
as the painter knew who stretched out his poet
at the edge of a canvas
declining to look back into a landscape.

# Remembering Summer
*For Stephen Spender*

I was one of those children
in an elementary school classroom
your parents in the rich house kept you from
I learned to love your thighpyloned landscape
with furry propellers
coalboned financiers arming ambered ladies
skyblock churches
birdbursts of singing from young comrades
chimneysweeps and factory children caged
in history books
whose topsyturvy dog-god rhymes
you freed to beat for our cruel times

you walked out of your books
past a vineyard with cypresses where I saw sunrise
to Anamas
our summer house
a garden of grey olives
thyme and fennel
sprinkled with daisies and lizards
sunborn poet in a purple shirt
praising my daughters' looks
giving a hand with the poubelle
for midday greeting

tall and fair like you
Natasha meeting us
brown feet in dangling blue ropesoles
we were at home
you with a basin of hedge blackberries for dessert
and the sorcier
divining a lucky depth for your well
at Mas St. Jérome

the Milky Way frothed over our terrace at Anamas
mothy air and cool wine in companionable night
we joked at Auden's ignorance of stars
as Vega shone conspicuous for his love-feast
quoted the brilliance of a famous season
its poet known to you who knew them all
unimaginable zero summer
set flowering for midwinter spring

summer's done but I hear always
in our heartless days
the god-dog songs mouthed for illiterate kids
crawling through the bleak bluebooks

## Writing Woman

Her eye shines in her painter's eyes
absented
by his gaze
her back to the painted
wall
where a ship's sail swells
fanned by farewells
across unseen distances

as he lifts her look from the page
her pen grazes
trims the feather flying
in her right hand
rests her left hand on a grey velvet cloth
beside a string of small pearls
and a ribbon to bind bows in her plaited crown
above the big pearls
dangling from brown braids

plumps her billowy jacket of quilted silk
and brown-flecked milky ermine
and shines her face in a buttercup morning
which streams into the room's darkness
to flame table and sheet and body

he sees

she words
her longing
not seeing whose eye is freeing her blackeyed gaze
whose brush is busy with sparks of paint
in her eyes on her head and the skin of her pearls
and the little gilt pins stuck in starshapes
on the chair
where she writes her letter.

## Concerto for the Left Hand

Ravel wrote a concerto
for Wittgenstein
who returned from the war
onehanded.

The composer played his music to the pianist
who did not like it
took it away to make changes
then played it
saying
performers should not be slaves.

Ravel listened
did not like it
took it away and made changes
saying
performers are slaves.

When this masterpiece is played
– by Pascal Roget for example –
you cannot tell
only one hand is on the keys.

## At the Movies

sunset boulevard or long goodbye
framed limbs curl and clasp
you can't see the flushed features
but above the bed in black and white
the god and goddess face us
she keeps a bland eye on slack-muscled sleep
dimpled cherubs try on helmet and bucklers
all shiny and small inside their rectangle
while the coloured lovers are enormous
we know they are us
a thousand eyes beaming at the lit scenes
outside their dark a girl leans
on the wall gilded by exit
torch loose in fingers and lidded look telling
she has seen these screens a thousand times
lifts her head at the swelling notes
to yawn into the light again
as the sitters strut off like stars
eyes in the gallery frame her story
marking the crimson stripe of a blue suit
foxy glints of the soft seating
a painted dreamer or simply
a servant of the dream
ushered home to a cold bed
or urged into lovers' arms
to dream love-plays under a text or picture
of war or waves
icy alps or gods reproduced
in the glossy catalogue New York 1981
painted blonde
canvas and celluloid
thinned to a paper reading
till hankering after small truths
dying to escape artifice
true love begs artfully for lies
a lying truthteller shuts up
small talk and print
to turn into a present

whose rain dries on grey pavements
to step in the here and now
as it becomes the now and then
cautious or clever or simply
at home knowing the hazards of home
a cat on the catwalk catching
at the tailend split second
before it fades into a framing.

## The Letter

You know I never wrote much of a letter
unlike you
and when I tell you things are getting better
that's really true

but I can't put my feelings in a letter
they're not amusing
even if knowing them made you feel better
I always found confessing too confusing.

I'd tell you if I knew where I was going
I really would
and if these are wild oats that I've been sowing
perhaps I could

but I could never tell what crops were growing
in the fine weather
and didn't even know where we were going
when we were going there together.

## Had It Been a Dream

They left in the middle of the dance
out of heat into cold
out of a garden into fields
beating through undergrowth

bushes and clawing thorn
to the crossroads
where an inn's open door
lit a welcome

fire and wine
she sharpened words to stab
he stared in his glass and said
this is how things come to an end

had it been a dream
we could have gone
on to the heart of the pathless wood
to wake at the shriek of light
astonished by day's embrace.

# Dogwood

No slow unfolding
These buds rip apart
Tender bracts green as leaves
Bleed at the tip
To scar in the sun's cure

Goldcrowned
Foursquare
This flower forgoes perfection
Pink or white it stays stained
From its rough birthing
Until its withering

# No Shadow

Today's loving casts no shadow
As we lie tamed in aftermath
Bodies touching without fever
Cradled easy in the hollow
Left by the manylimbed big dancer
Who trembles with delighted tantrum
To urge us into weightlessness.

The nonchalant angels arrange it
Muffle the drumbeats of the city
Calm the heartthrob of the clocks
Drain the colours from the garden
So that we see no shadow
When the afternoon light dwindles
To shrink the circle that contains us.

# The Champagne Eclipse

*For Josephine, Julie, Christopher, Wyndham, Evelyn, Nathan and Kate,*
*Helston, August 11, 1999*

The Lizard festival beat time
we filed through grass and ploughland
with our improvised equipment
the dancing boys dodging live wires
to try a wall or gate's viewpoint
all staring out the grey cloud cover

we counted down to blackout
till at the zero second
weather cleared round the high sun
and with a glimpse of light turned night we ducked
to watch mirrored in box and bucket
glittering shifts of disc and crescent

sky darkened
quickening a ripple in the blood
a second day broke in the east
and round the whole horizon
birds and distant drums broke silence
we cried miracle and drank to ancient science.

## Something Self-Contained

I am looking for somewhere to live
but you are not with me
as I search the long streets
for a place where we can be together
two rooms with a separate entrance
private and quiet but not too dear
no need for garden or terrace
just something selfcontained.

The move took no time at all
narrow rooms lead out of each other
to a mirrored twisting passage
deep alcoves and ticking clock
the Hamadan rug spread by the fire
pictures hung and a table laid
the rainbow quilt woven in Wales
on the bed where a lamp is shining

by the green velvet chair we never bought
that cashmere shawl I left in a cab
black and white cups and saucers shining
the coffee set smashed in the post
our wedding present from your mother
I am puzzled by loneliness
somebody's laughing outside the door
and there's no comfort in the company.

## The Marriage of Miranda

I wanted Caliban not Ferdinand
but as he fingered my virginity
a father's magic took me by the hand

where waves whipped up a whirlwind on demand
to pluck a pearl of princes from the sea
I wanted Caliban not Ferdinand

when they set up a chessboard on the sand
and with cold ceremony mated me
a father's magic took me by the hand

as wordless music I cannot withstand
assures me in the language of a cry
I wanted Caliban not Ferdinand

their brave new world I cannot understand
above my head Ariel is flying free
I wanted Caliban not Ferdinand
a father's magic took me by the hand.

# Gertrude's Villanelle

Your father's footsteps echo in your head
You follow them as if you were a boy
We must be done with dreaming of the dead

He haunts a son but shuns his widow's bed
The heyday in the blood brought him no joy
Your father's footsteps echo in your head

They echoed for the girl he came to wed
Stern martial drumbeats pounding to destroy
We must be done with dreaming of the dead

I shed my black to see fresh bakemeats spread
Crying, le roi est mort, vive le roi
Your father's footsteps echo in your head

The lute is strung to wind the dancers' thread
The song insists in order to enjoy
We must be done with dreaming of the dead

Embrace flesh and be deaf to the ghost's tread
Its rhyme and rhythm sound a grave's decoy
Your father's footsteps echo in your head
We must be done with dreaming of the dead

## The Dowry

I am my dowry
Precious and unpriced
After the crossing
From my father's country
To your shore
That promised better where
After my losing
A breaking wave
Is still beating

Bringing nothing
Love must be emptyhanded

Eyes washed with weeping
See the more clearly
Unprized and prizing
In my father's house
Now this revealing
Flesh and bone opening
To you here
In hurt and healing

Bringing nothing
Love must be emptyhanded

I leave grieving
My father's kingdom
Heart's truth cutting
Halved between you two
No less and no more
There will be warring
Before homecoming
For birds on the tree
Who cannot stay singing

Bringing nothing
Love must be emptyhanded

## Steeplechase

If we could halt the mare
in mid-air
before her rider clasps closer for his killing move

if we could bribe the bridegroom
in love with innocence
make him listen as she longs to break the silence

if the lovers could hold the embrace
sing out joy face to face
drown the madbrain's promise to storm their music

if we had not watched the careful clocks
left the crumpled bed
to a room's emptiness

if all the beggars were choosers
Frou-frou would fall in some other race
and lovers still be losers

yet always there's the longing
to lift the noose from her head
gag slander
set a chair for you at my deathbed
and cheer on the mare
to win the steeplechase.

## The Grandmother's Story

Stand still, my darling, as I brush your hair,
look at our reflections there, in the long mirror,
gold and silver.

Fifty brush-strokes for a husband, a hundred for a lover.
Maria used to say that when she brushed my hair,
my mother's maid, poor Maria
her head was filled with wise saws and silly songs
every night she lulled
me to sleep with ballads and old tales.

She never had a husband, and her lover left her,
the old story,
she went off one day and never came back,
I never saw her again,
no, I never heard what happened, only the whispering.

The first time she put up my hair
binding a white lily in the braided knot
it was for a grand dinner
in honour of the Russian ambassador.
I'd been anxious and busy all day, and she soothed me,
put her hands on my shoulders,
smiling at our faces close together
in this long mirror.

We had a houseful of servants
but our old housekeeper was getting frail
and since mother's death I saw to everything.
Father was very particular,
everything had to be perfect.

I am wearing a white silk dress,
the lily in my hair,
yes, Mother's pearls warm round my throat,
silver and rose glitter on the long table
under flakes of crystal.

On my right is a foreigner,
a soldier who spends his life travelling.
His voice binds me in its telling,
in his eyes a sword glitters,
jungles and glaciers, deserts and volcanoes,
slaves and treasure.
A third of his finger points the measure
of a woman's bound foot.
My drawn breath hurts.

Other faces dissolve to mist,
other voices are sea in a shell.
Then the binding spell
breaks
I catch my aunt's eye and stumble to my feet.
I twist the butterfly silk of my dress
crushing it.

My world is a house.

Up the curled stairway the women flutter
to mirrors and maids and drawing-room chatter
of diamonds and illness, weddings and dress,
birth and adultery.
They admire the sea-green tapestry
worked by my grandmother,
maiden bound by monster,
some Ariadne or Andromeda.
A soar of laughter from the men at their wine.

It is late when they join us,
I talk to a white-haired judge, who danced with my grandmother,
she also wore a white ball-dress
and as he praises my likeness
I hear my father and the ambassador
talking to the traveller,
Father urges him to visit us,
'My house is yours'
but he never came back.

No, I never saw him again.
Funny, I hadn't thought of him for years.
Funny how things come back,
desires and tears
flushed out from the dark
by some little thing, a mirror, a handkerchief, a hair-brush,
yes, I can see his dark heavy face
slashed
by a scar from ear to nose.

There, I've finished,
off you go, your hair's shining,
see if you can find a husband or lover
as handsome as your grandfather.
Our marriage was made in our cradles,
our fathers were old friends,
we were very happy.

# The Peacock Screen

The old king drew his last breath sweetly
On the satin pillow the seamstress embroidered
In sprays of pale elder and honeysuckle

Gold threads sparked in the flamy folds
Of the swirling silks she sewed for the dancer
Whose wildfire wheeled on whirling points

Kingfisher wing slanted beryl to emerald
In the coat she stitched for the young king's wedding
To a white girl whose skin was sun on water

He ordered a screen to be made for his bride
So her needle flashed its finedrawn colours
To show the mating of the palace peacocks

Beside the drab brown of the little peahen
Eyes of bronze and viridian glittering
Spread the great glossy fan of his gorgeous tailfeathers

She laboured over the lacetraced gown
Softened with swansdown for the christening
Threads drawn and cut for bud and honeycomb

Coralpoint, snowpoint, and stitches in air
She twisted the fine mesh round her wrist
To dye it deep in the blood of her cutwork.

# Lullaby

Go back to sleep now
The dreams will be sweet ones
Hair spread on white linen
Gold brushed into silk

I was a baby
When they buried my mother
Her waitingmaid nursed me
And warmed me with love

Her own child was stillborn
She stripped off her clothing
Cried for her lover
Sang her mad songs

They clothed her and fed her
Put me to her cold breast
To drink the sweet milk
And warm her with love

As I grew older
She lulled me with soft songs
Told me her stories
Brushed my gold hair

When I was twenty
Your father came riding
Out of the forest
To warm me with love

He brought me wild flowers
Put pearls round my white throat
Turned dance to embracing
Sang love's sweet song

The day we were married
She was not there to dress me
To bind up my long hair
And dance at the wedding

She ran into the forest
Stripped off her clothing
Sang her mad songs
Embraced the cold river

Go back to sleep now
The bad dream is over
When you wake in the morning
The birds will be singing

## The Locked Chest

I tried the lid of the lacquered chest
that stood in a corner of my room
but mother stopped my hand and said
the time for opening would come soon.

They took my brother to hunt the boar
he came back with a wounded thigh
groaned on his bed for a week and a day
and to my tears made no reply.

A golden key shone in the lock
I turned it and lifted the heavy lid,
scent of cedar sweetened the box
and I found a ring and a sheet inside.

I unfurled the fine bleached cloth and it
wrapped around me like a cloak
smoothly I slipped on the ring.
my finger swelled and my nail turned black.

I begged her to unwind the linen
ease off the tightened band
bring cool water from the spring
to bathe the crimson weal on my hand

but mother smiled and shook her head
as I wore the sheet and the ring
my skin would heal and the scar fade
it was time for the opening.

## On the Train

They got in at Port Talbot
she was fair and fat
he was dark and skinny with a pigtail
he said she was a big six and could go to the toilet alone
she said wheedling no only a baby six
asked how long his book was
he said a hundred and ninety pages
she conjured from a blue bag
Barbie in a white bed
a fluffy pony Roseandaisy
Spike the dragon
a monster called Lovecrayon
a baby with windup handle in his stomach
bottle and baby-sitter
how many stops to London?
do you live in a flat or a house? have you been to Ponyland?
who is in charge of the trains? all the trains?
the rest of us pretending
to read or look out of the window
he said the Engaged sign meant
a promise to get married
she said he was bananas
balancing a plastic wedding cake on Roseandaisy's head
said he could borrow it
do you love Jane? enough to marry her?
what colour is the carpet in your livingroom? a carpet or a mat?
you know without my mother
you wouldn't have a daughter?
has my mother gone back to Walter?
when we get to your flat
can we leave a message on her answerphone saying we love her?
he said we'll say Beck and I arrived safely
she's having a good time
when we get to Paddington
can we have our photograph taken
in the little cabinet
when we get
to your house can we play tapes and watch Casualty?
is there a bridge
between your house and my mother's?

## Changing Trains

They sat alone during the railway journey
no one watching as they watched each other's faces
never touching and not breaking the silence
while an old dilemma longed to be dissolved
tunnels deepened and signals resolved.

They never arrived at their destination
their remains were recovered from the wreckage
then identified by close relations
one was buried and one cremated
other passengers survived without a scratch.

They changed trains at the frontier station
then travelled to her birthplace in the mountains
where no-one pressed him to tell his story
he soon acquired the dialect of the region
though he was never happy with the curfew.

They journeyed on without changing trains
unhampered by passport control or customs
flew across an ocean to his city
where she learnt to breathe in the conditioned air
and smiled as she talked to the computers.

The strategy of farewell had its successes
when the train stopped and he handed down her luggage
went on waving very slowly from the window
as she crossed over to the other platform
to rehearse the embraces of homecoming.

They did not speak to their fellow passengers,
looked out at crossing lines and earthen cuttings
did not touch and did not break the silence.
An old dilemma longed to be resolved
as cities shifted and landscape dissolved.

## Globe

I dust the old world
birthday present
from a shop by St Paul's
twirled like a wineglass
while we marvelled at all the sea.

Ice roughens grass
I pack sundresses
for a flight into summer.

Safe and sound
in a stranger's hands
in no time
I touch ground.

The postwoman in New South Wales
assembles on the counter
as I warm in her peculiar sun
a world jigsaw
lifts my letter from the scales
for its trip into winter
says land's done
but the sea will take some time.

# Refugee

Father would take grandfather on his back
we children carry food and the hearthgods
who join future to past and must be fed.
My older brother frowned and shook his head
for a weapon he needed the iron spade
my little brother pleaded with his eyes
hugging the tiny sword and wooden horse
my sister seized her staring painted doll
I took a last look at the family treasures,
the brocade robe mother had worn at feasts,
a slab of crystal found among the rocks
as we watched the enemy triremes slope off,
a bronze mirror, my grandmother's distaff,
her silver bucket on its gold-rimmed wheels,
bit my lip and shouldered bread and gods
coming down to the street of women's cries

unshed tears burning in my eyes
my big brother brandishing the shovel
the young one mimicking a soldier's march
Father urging us and striding fast ahead
in spite of the old man clutched round his neck
my leather burdens banging at my back
smoke and stonedust blistering our throats
we pushed on in the crush for the west gates
to get clear of the shattered citadels
where we'd played at boobytraps and chariots
in earshot of a bloody battlefield,
intent now on the river and mountains
and beyond them to some sanctuary or refuge –
I thought yes you could call us refugees
but just as I was trying my new word
my brother tripped and fell on his toy sword,
bending to help I stumbled and cried out
the bag of gods swung hard against my breast
my ankle twisted in the ashy cobbles

and father shouted that we must keep up
'Can't have you falling back in this mad mob'.

But I knew I'd never manage with the weight.
I could only go on if I travelled light
and mother's frayed whimpering spirit
imploring me to guard the little gods
nourished by all our sacred ancestors
never touched by any hand bloodied in wars
was silenced by a rough and older voice
by the cold reason of the refugee

so as we passed the temple of Apollo
I tipped the load of gods behind a pillar
and gave a hand to my brother and my sister.

# In No Named Place

Summer and winter we'd be up at dawn
in the V8 or old Mercedes heading west
our earliest mapmarks an Esso sign
and a new factory's yellow pyramid
the kids singsonging as they woke
in crazy sleeptime 'Is Swansea in London?'
and 'Is that Grannie's house?'
mooing to brown cows cwching down for rain
'Are you Gower cows, mae'n bwrw glaw heddiw'
counting red cars, spring lambs or Christmas trees,
piecing an alphabet from the signposts
unriddling Cirencester and Gloucester
savouring chips and the view from Birdlip
counting green bottles and men gone to mow
passing old mines in the Forest of Dean
to find the Brecon Beacons darkening
sun still brilliant on the English side
shimmying along the head of valleys' road
up and down Merthyr's black streets
by the slagheap and pits
swopping our childhood's bad thirties
in South Wales and South Shields
on the high narrow road by Senni Bridge
stopping to hear the flat cracked Sunday bells
of drowned towns deep down in the reservoir
always mapping some new crossing place
until they slung a silver road up high
a wiry tightrope over the fierce tide

and 'I won't go on that' one child declared
'No, just look at the waves' her sister cried
'the river's swirling and terribly wide
I'll keep my eyes tight shut till we're across'
so they sat hunched unmoving and wordless
until we reached the Welsh side and I said

'See, all safe now on the dry land
the new bridge held us and we're nearly home.'

On the way back I saw my mirrored frown
I had to cross the airy bridge on foot
on my own
stop somewhere in the middle
to look down at the quick brown tide
from the narrow footway or a dream
in no named country.

Funny things, bridges,
stone, wicker, wood, iron, steel, Roman, Victorian, modern,
humpbacked, roofed, suspended, pile-driven
over the Connecticut, Cothi, Thames, Tawe and Severn.

# OTHER BOOKS FROM SHOESTRING PRESS

MORRIS PAPERS: Poems Arnold Rattenbury. Includes 5 colour illustrations of Morris's wallpaper designs. "The intellectual quality is apparent in his quirky wit and the skilful craftsmanship with which, for example, he uses rhyme, always its master, never its servant." *Poetry Nation Review.*

ISBN 1 899549 03 X          £4.95

INSIDE OUTSIDE: NEW AND SELECTED POEMS Barry Cole. "A fine poet ... the real thing." *Stand.*

ISBN 1 899549 11 0          £6.95

COLLECTED POEMS Ian Fletcher. With Introduction by Peter Porter. Fletcher's work is that of "a virtuoso", as Porter remarks, a poet in love with "the voluptuousness of language" who is also a master technician.

ISBN 1 899549 22 6          £8.95

A COLD SPELL: Angela Leighton. The first full collection by a much admired poet.

ISBN: 1 899549 40 4          £6.95

TESTIMONIES: NEW AND SELECTED POEMS Philip Callow. With Introduction by Stanley Middleton. A generous selection whch brings together work from all periods of the career of this acclaimed novelist, poet and biographer.

STONELAND HARVEST: NEW AND SELECTED POEMS Dimitris Tsaloumas. This generous selection brings together poems from all periods of Tsaloumas's life and makes available for the first time to a UK readership the work of this major Greek-Australian poet.

ISBN 1 8995549 35 8          £8.00

ODES Andreas Kalvos. Translated into English by George Dandoulakis. The first English version of the work of a poet who is in some respects the equal of his contemporary, Greece's national poet, Solomos.

ISBN 1 899549 21 8          £9.95

LANDSCAPES FROM THE ORIGIN AND THE WANDERING OF YK Lydia Stephanou. Translated into English by Philip Ramp. This famous book-length poem by one of Greece's leading poets was first published in Greece in 1965. A second edition appeared in 1990.

ISBN 1 899549 20 X          £8.95

POEMS Manolis Anagnostakis. Translated into English by Philip Ramp. A wide-ranging selection from a poet who is generally regarded as one of Greece's most important living poets and who in 1985 won the Greek State Prize for Poetry.

ISBN 1 899549 19 6          £8.95

THE FREE BESIEGED AND OTHER POEMS Dionysios Solomos
In English versions. Edited by Peter Mackridge.

ISBN 1 899549 41 2          £8.00

SELECTED POEMS Tassos Denegris. Translated into English by Philip Ramp. A
generous selection of the work of a Greek poet with an international reputation.
Denegris's poetry has been translated into most major European languages and he has
read across the world.

ISBN 1 899549 45 9          £6.95

THE FIRST DEATH Dimitris Lyacos. Translated into English by Shorsha Sullivan.
With six masks by Friedrich Unegg. Praised by the Italian critic Bruno Rosada for
"the casting of emotion into an analytical structure and its distillation into a means
of communication", Lyacos's work has already made a significant impact across
Europe, where it has been performed in a number of major cities.

ISBN 1 899549 42 0          £6.95

Books of related interest from Trent Editions

**Robert Bloomfield:** *The Selected Poems of Robert Bloomfield*

Edited by John Goodridge and John Lucas, Intro. by John Lucas

Robert Bloomfield (1766–1823), was the most successful of the self-taught 'peasant
poets' of the Romantic period, a prolific and popular writer whose first book *The
Farmer's Boy* (1800), sold an unprecedented 26,000 copies in three years, and won
the praise of Wordsworth, and John Clare, who called him the 'English Theocritus'.
In the 20th century Edmund Blunden, among others, was a great admirer of
Bloomfield.
This edition includes a selection of Bloomfield's prose prefaces, as well as
explanatory notes, a chronology of Bloomfield's life and a list of further reading.

Price: £7.99 ISBN 0 905 48894 6

**William Barnes:** *The Poems of William Barnes*

Edited, with a critical commentary, by Val Shepherd

William Barnes (1801–1886) is justly renowned for poems which, using their own
Dorset dialect, speak out for the agricultural labouring families of the nineteenth-
century Blackmoor Vale. Many of these expressions of village and private life
appear in this Trent Edition but, in addition, a selection of the little known poems
that Barnes wrote in Standard English is also included.

Price: £7.99 ISBN 0 905 48895 4

**John Clare:** *John Clare: the Living Year*

Edited, with an introduction and notes, by Tim Chilcott.

1841 was one of the most productive, varied, and imaginatively moving periods of John Clare's long poetic career. Against a background of asylum, escape home, and then forced removal to a second asylum, he wrote during this single year over 3,000 lines of original poetry and paraphrase, in addition to a substantial body of prose.

Price: £7.99 ISBN 0 905 488 55 5

## from GREENWICH EXCHANGE

WILDERNESS: 36 POEMS 1972–93 Martin Seymour-Smith. Admired by other poets from Robert Graves to Ian Hamilton, Martin Seymour-Smith was a poet of unfailing craft who combined an astringent wit with a deep regard for the joys and pains of being alive.

ISBN 1 871551 08 0          £6.00

All these books may be ordered through Shoestring Press, 19 Devonshire Avenue, Beeston, Nottingham NG9 1BS. Tele/fax 0115 9251827.